Scarlet Antiquities

Tales of Lives Macarbe

Nathan Pereira

BookLeaf
Publishing

India | USA | UK

Made with ❤ on the BookLeaf Publishing Platform
www.bookleafpub.in
www.bookleafpub.com

Dedication

"For those yearning for a dash of fantasy & a spice of the dark.
Grim realities may not be human after all..."

To my family and friends, my closest supporters
cherished confidants and pillars of strength...

A special thanks to my proof readers and muses
the world is crazy for we are sane...

Preface

This collection contains a collection in itself. Of tales and
myths spoken by friends.
Speak with the poet and his collection of poems,
detailing lives not far from our own. Filled with mystery
and told with wit, do ponder it over, for it has merit.
If proses are more to your taste, the chronicler has tales
encased. Myths and folklore brought to life, haunting
memories, solemn strife.
Or ease into plays of the actor. Something new and
exciting every step you gather.
A curious collection marked by grim undertone
A wonderful collection for all to own.

Acknowledgements

Its a shame for a poet to walk alone, lucky am I to be surrounded by many people who care for me.
I would like to thank my teachers and parents for inculcating the joy of reading into me. This joy was the soil on which my writing passion started to take root and has now flourished into a towering tree, trying to spread the same joy to others.

I would also like to thank my friends and proof readers for staying with me and supporting me during my times of self doubt. Your encouragement and constant presence have been a constant source of my passion. Without your assistance I would have given up when facing any one of my numerous writing blocks.

A special thanks to my muses. You guys were a constant source of motivation and inspiration. The joy of penning the thoughts we shared was as frightening as it was gratifying.

I would also like thank bookleaf publication for giving

me a chance to realise my dream and become a published author in 2025.

1. The Poet

"Curious is it not
To be haunted by the mundane?
Plagued by wonder
A hint of the arcane....

Curious yet
To know a tale?
One filled with scenes
Not meant for the frail...

Curse of the mind
Or truth hidden from the blind?
A conundrum truly
One of a kind...

To see the lives
Of souls departed,
Their memories filling
Objects discarded...

For there is something yet
Hidden away
Like shadows playing
On a summer day...

So listen well
To these tales of mine..
For there is wonder yet
In things left behind..."

1.a. The Book

A quiet place, covers enwind
Filled with knowledge
Cursed with time...

Away from its ethereal lair
Hides a book O so rare
Naked when watched by sight
Filled with ink after a human bite

For none know of fates loom
Many afraid of eternal doom
The curse of cherished womb
To lay buried in forgotten tomb...

A cautionary tale O reader of mine
If you find a story so fine
Blurring the lines set by fate
A vision seared
By pearly gates

Is it decreed
Or is it earned?
A life lived
A story laid
Or was it I
Who was betrayed…

1.b. The Coin

Work for a fee, never for free
For such is the way of the world...

Man kills man,
Cares not for kin or clan
A land for his hubris...

Work for a fee, never for free
For such is the way of the world...

A new task, a new command
Locked in bones and skull
Perish in mortal struggle

Work for me, never set free
For such is the way of the world...

Woken again with ivory skin
An abomination, an unholy sin
We long to make them suffer

Against our plea, defying the sisters three
For such is the way of the world...

Called again, there is no end
man has met the crooner
Where O where is your ruler...

Cry out fate, scream destiny,
For such is the way of the world...

1.c. The Scales

Another Day, Another Failure
Wonderful day to wander in nature
Away from the schemes and machinations of man
Worth nothing in this lifespan
But the scales are always equal....

Another illness, another crime
Another day where I am not worth a dime
A lonely village, a deadly plague
Nature gives and nature takes
For the scales are always equal

Another house, another bride
Another child wailing in the night
Pity family will never see
A life filled with glee
But the scales are always equal

Another human, another sin
Another reason to blame fate's kin

Man scared of nature's wrath
My name, a curse spat
For the scales are always equal

1.d. The Statue

"For alone i lay
In void and strife
Stolen from the colors of life

Taken from sight,
Fancied a flight
Only to fall and
Break under might...

Bereft of sound
shackled and bound
Sword and hammer
Soak the ground

Vanished of Scent
Dreams of ascent
Broken and battered
Forced to lament

Reaved of taste

A fleeting embrace
In this world
Without passion or grace

Deprived of touch
Content to rush
Crushing hope
It is a crutch...

Alone i lay
In void and strife
Stolen from the colors of life"

1.e. The Mirror

"An inch here,
A feet there,
The Soil has acres to spare...

A drop here
A sip there
The Seas are never bare

A breath here
A breeze there
The Skies are always fair

An ember here
A spark there
Surely no cause for despair

No grain here
No land there
Scrambling to hide from nature's tear

No life here
No water there
Seething are seas beware

No wisps here
No echoes there
Solace is found nowhere ”

1.f. The Crown

Broken stone
We moan and groan
Always a shade of monotone
For we Chip, Chip and Break Away...

Forced to drown
In a life of frowns
Longing to wear the crown
For we Chip, Chip and Break Away...

Sharpen and hone
Your grit and bone
Sword's curse, forever alone
For we Chip, Chip and Break Away...

Victors but a fateful clown
One possessing some renown
Spending days in coffin brown
For we Chip, Chip and Break Away...

2. The Chronicler

Solemn Silence
All I ask from readers of mine
To make the story completely thine
For the ink tells one and words the other
Lying in wait for you to discover

Subdued Silence
All I ask from readers of mine
To understand the stories design
For the lips read one and speak the other
Lying in wait for you to uncover

Sustained silence
All I ask from readers of mine
To decipher the clues and the signs
For the eyes see one and gaze the other
Lying in wait for you to gather

Soft Silence
All I ask from readers of mine

To break it down and to refine
For the heart to feel and mind to endear
Hoping to last forever...

2.a. The Rag

There was a little child
Left alone without a guide
He was for this
banished and reviled
Cast away, forgotten aside.

Filled with love and melody inside
Fangs of society had him defiled
Watched to suffer, made to abide

The child grew quick
The child grew fast
The innocence was stripped at last
Forced to learn from rags and ills
Finding melodies in haunting shrills

There was once a little child
Grown to be a withering plight
Leading and beguiling the exiled,
A heathen, a scourge, A nightmare bright

There was once a little child...

2.b. The Bow

A hunter hunts only his prey
Respecting the earth, following its way
Hunt for hunger, satiate your thirst
A simple life, joy coerced...

A hunter finds broken kin
Scattered dust, bloodied skin
Wet eyes gaze on scarlet ground
A simple life, now oath-bound

A hunter tracks down his prey
His life shattered, a dull gray
A solitary goal left ahead
A simple life, living dead

A hunter spots his target with kin
Reason away, the oath begins
Curses fly and so do limbs
A simple life, haunting hymns

A hunter hunts out of craze
Butchering lands, stuck in daze
Waking Blight, maddening dreams
A simple life, filled with screams...

2.c. The Cats

Oh how I love my cats
Their moody nature and how their tail wags
Did you know they have nine lives
What a joy it would be to be a cat

We had a nasty surprise today
Furballs, furballs everywhere....
And no food....
No food to share...
Where are my cats today ?

We found a tail today,
The cats let me borrow one of theirs
I wonder when we will get food today
Maybe I should step outside
Should I take my cats?

I have been a bad bad cat
My husband doesn't understand
He tried to separate me from my cats

I only scratched him for while
He drenched me red, that made me smile
Maybe i am a cat

The humans are so silly
Asking about a human to a cat
Why do I smell a rat ?
My husband is such a delicious view
Just rip and tear and chew
Oh how i love to be a cat.....

2.d. The Shears

A mansion lays far up the hill
A grim reminder a solemn chill
For the gates are meant to keep the monster in
A curse of god in human skin...

The grounds are but perilous test
The shears flying, devil's jest
For every year on the phantasmal eve
The mansion grants him its leave...

Descending down, with a voice so deep
Akin to disaster rising from hallows keep
"Time to reap and Time to grow
The grounds lay in amusing throe..."

"Time to prune and time to wander
Not a moment left to squander
To snip and snap and snip again
The grounds covered in ..."

"Maybe the years have made me fonder
For sometimes i am left to ponder
The insides of man are a curious sight
Their squeals are such a delight
So I snip and snap and snip again
For the joy of innocent pain"

2.e. The Razor

Scissors, comb and a razor
A gaunt man, a crisp blazer
An empty store, a haunting figure
Surely there is no danger?
Scissors, Comb and a razor

A quiet nod, a practiced gait
"Welcome Sir to this saloon of mine,
A workshop almost divine.
Pray tell what gets you in so late,"
Surely I am in no danger ?
Scissors, Comb and a razor

Astonished still my body betrays
Moving stiffly while my mind downplays
The absurdity of the situation I face
"Worry not sir and rest your mind..."
Everything seems hazy, my minds in a daze
Why did I walk in here ?
Scissors, comb and a razor

"Delicate skin in a man so rare
Luscious and Bountiful hair....
Your face is such a delight to wear
Surely you do not mind Sir
I pose no danger..... "
Scissors, comb and a razor

2.f. The Rose

Gather round for roses red
Cut fresh from nature's bed
For maidens young and to be wed
Blossoming love but words unsaid
Gather round for roses red

A patron nay a lover true
Come hither and take a view
A mystery, A wonder and A clue
A selection of only the finest few
Gather round for roses new

Come inside and take a gander still
To see my roses grow and enthrill
A reminder of my rose's will
Do hurry and spare the winter chill
Gather round while roses spill

Oh did i give you a scare

Worry not bout the cadavers stare
She's but a maiden bare
My roses broodmare
Gather round for my roses fair

Gather round for roses red
A pity that you shall be bled
Roses blooming from a beautiful head
Such a tale is sure to spread
Gather round for my roses red

3. The Actor

"Who am I
Nay who are you
A child grown on promises untrue?

Who am I
Nay who are you
A youth filled with shadows undue?

Who am I
Nay who are you
An adult hiding secrets taboo?

Who am I
Nay who are you
An elder hiding from death's pursue?

A soldier then
Through war and strife
Surely not against his wife...

A lover then
Filled with passion and trust
Surely not a cover for lust...

Maybe a scholar
Learned and wise
Surely not a profession of lies

Who am I
Nay who are you
But an actor waiting for cue... ”

3.a. The Bells

Marriage bells are ringing
The choir is singing
O what joy it is
For you to see

The pastor and his faithful
The groom quite deceitful
For the snakes have snitch
The brides a witch
Oh the bride is me....

The owls and crows are screeching
The air has started freezing
Oh what joyous wedding
It'll be...

The march of the hateful
The laughter of the sinful
For the curse has spread
While, blood has shed

Oh the hall erupts with glee

The groom lays down bleeding
The faithful crying and screaming
Body and mind, alone and apart
The wondrous joy of beautiful art

For the marriage bells are ringing
The fires are a'singing
The joyous wedding of you and me...

3.b. The Lamp

Never again never again
Shall the spirits lead me astray
Why does my mind betray
My body in disarray
Why are the lamps so inane?

Move again Move again
Worry not by the passer's gaze
Filling life with shallow praise
Bickering bout another craze
Do the lamps share my disdain ?

Staring again Staring again
Smiling at my plight
Banished from beauty bright
Cursed to wander the endless night
Is it time for lamps to unchain?

Brighter still brighter still
The bodies yet remain

Lived mundane

Died insane

Burn again without restrain....

3.c. The Watch

One two three four
A quiet house
A frozen door
One two three four

One two three
A wailing plea
A quiet glee
A murder spree
One two three

One and two
I made a stew
A homely brew
Scrumptious sight
But tough to chew
One and two

Only one
I had my fun

the tale has just begun
You can hide and
You can run
Yet night follows the rising sun...

3.d. The Net

Solemn water, lonely boat
A man sailing in seas remote
Nothing more than watery ditch

The net is cast
As in the days past
Hoping for fins and scales.

The man is shocked
When net is docked
Carrying coffers rich.

The net is flung
For greed has stung
Dreaming of royal hails

The ropes have bound
A harrowing sound
Seas scratching a pesky itch

The net is lowered
The seas have devoured
Another glutton pales...

3.e. The Blade

Run away O' run away
Here comes the lady fair
Hide away O' hide away
Darkness is her pair...

Run away O' run away
The madness whispers loud
Hide away O' hide away
She wears the reaper's shroud

Run away O' run away
The blade thirsts for blood
Hide away O' hide away
Its time for death to flood

Run away O' run away
The Spider lays in wait
Hide away O' hide away
You have sealed your fate

Running away O' Running away
A gift lands at my feet
Hiding away O' Hiding away
The heart tastes so sweet...

3.f. The Flag

Oh ho ho
Oh ho ho
A sailor comes from land afar
A blade, a musk, a bulging scar
To find a shrine
The stars align
Waiting for death to call

Oh ho ho
Oh ho ho
A sailor enters the local bar
A nap, a snack, a flowin jar
He found the shrine
He stole a dime
Waiting for death to call

Oh ho ho
Oh ho ho
A sailor flees thru bazaar
A sack full of things bizarre

He sailed away
From traitor's bay
Waiting for death to call

Oh ho ho
Oh ho ho
A sailor stuck on seas
His crew dying of disease
Cursed to sway
Slaving away
Waiting for death to call